County Council

Libraries, books and more . . .

6·1·13	0 6 DEC 2012	
2 8 MAR 2013		

Please return/renew this item by the last due date.
Library items may be renewed by phone on
030 33 33 1234 (24 hours) or via our website
www.cumbria.gov.uk/libraries

Cumbria Libraries

CLIC

Interactive Catalogue

Ask for a CLIC password

THE CASUAL PERFECT

LAVINIA GREENLAW

The Casual Perfect

faber and faber

First published in 2011
by Faber and Faber Ltd
Bloomsbury House
74–77 Great Russell Street
London WC1B 3DA

Typeset by Faber and Faber Ltd
Printed in England by T. J. International Ltd, Padstow, Cornwall

The right of Lavinia Greenlaw to be identified as author
of this work has been asserted in accordance with Section 77
of the Copyright, Designs and Patents Act 1988

A CIP record for this book
is available from the British Library

ISBN 978–0–571–27816–9

2 4 6 8 10 9 7 5 3 1

for Jonathan Reekie

Acknowledgements

Aldeburgh Music, Artevents, Barbican Centre, BBC Radio 3 and 4, Bookworks, Régis Cochefert, *Daedalus*, EPSRC/Performing Arts Labs, *Granta*, *Guardian*, *London Review of Books*, *Loops*, *Oxford Broadsides*, *Poetry* (USA), *Poetry Review*, Southbank Centre, *Times Literary Supplement*.

The original version of 'Einstein' was commissioned by the Science Museum to mark the centenary of the Theory of Relativity. 'Slow Passage, Low Prospect' was written as a song cycle, composed by Richard Baker; he also set 'The Lost Letter' and 'Song' as part of a concert aria ('Written on a Train') and 'English Lullaby' for *The NMC Songbook*. 'Winter Finding' was commissioned by Ian Wilson as the inspiration for his orchestral work of the same name.

I would like to thank Maura Dooley, David Harsent and Paul Keegan. Also Tim Dee and Paul Dodgson for our radio journeys, and Sandra Barry for her help and hospitality in Nova Scotia.

Contents

She thanked hym of al that he wel mente
Towardes hire . . .

THE CASUAL PERFECT

Essex Kiss

A handbrake turn on a hair-pin bend.
Merry-go-round? No, the waltzer.
A touch as bold as rum and peppermint.
Chewing gum and whelks, a whiff
of diesel, crocus, cuckoo spit.
The moves of a half-broken pony.
A poacher's tickle and snare.
I will lay you down
on a bed of nettles and blackthorn.
Your body will give way like grain,
your body will veer:
smoke over a torched field
as the wind takes and turns it.
The grip of bluebells.
The grip of wattle and daub.
As near as twelve lay-bys,
as far as a Friday night lock-in.
By this are we bound.
No paperwork.

Superlocution

Recently met, they intended to speak
of their landscapes and people.
Yet so deep a recognition
(as of the self's engine) took hold,
they cast their truth and secrets.

There is a way into the mountain.
It opens and closes and comes to rest
beneath the bed of a river. Yourself
as slow and sudden as rock.
Above – listen! – the hidden continuous.

The Casual Perfect

A borrowed tense.
Achievement of the provisional.

Paraphasia.
A gesture made in musical time.

The unarticled world.
A lapsed geography.

Description in action.
Her rooms somehow always at sea.

A childhood home.
The sprawling brightness of the return.

The intimacy of the telescope.
The becoming of quartz or iron.

Coleridge

So great a storm I rose in the night,
my mind in the hills, a dream of lateness.
What was it in my countenance
that made them harness thirty horses?
When at last they pulled together
we travelled with such speed and force
the driver threw the reins aside:
'Everything that's for us is against us.
We're going nowhere tonight.'

Kata

A dance between movement and space,
between image and imperative.
Each step an arrival
of the familiar within the unknown.
The gravity of form
and the mechanism of each gesture
as profound and dissolved
as the body's memory of a stranger
who said nothing but in passing
met with you in stillness
wanting to go no faster than this.

Empty Metaphor

The last room was a hall of mirrors
where my child stepped past.

Nineteen – about to be described
and yet to meet her explanation.

At the point of exchange
she became so unknown, so clear

that I could not tell glass from air.

Saturday Night

Out of the impenetrable wood
— ELIZABETH BISHOP

And young girls shall gather
to dance on the highway
under petals of light
that float from their shoulders
and dip into lotioned shadows.
They shall coil their salty hair
and tug at their lapsed muslins
as they fall like cushions, and spill.
Do they dance for those creatures
whose unmade selves
come unbuttoning out of the dark?
All strop and tang, they crave
whatever will settle their erupted
frames, their chemical blunders,
their overgrown sentences.
You who pass by can watch
but not enter the world of this place.
You know nothing of its way
of growing tree from shadow
so that all is fixed and root.
You who pass by, pass by.

The Literal Body

That for all her young womanhood
a broken instrument lodged in her jaw.

That in removing the sharp
they raised the roof of her mouth.

That her sight failed within a year
of being where she couldn't.

That when in love she suffers
a loss of sensation on the feminine side.

That what her body remembers most clearly
is being held by breaking glass.

That when in love she loses the ability
to digest.

That her skin is feathers
and her teeth are eggshell.

That she is knuckle and sinew.
That she is low.

That she is pale.

That in times of uncertainty
every doorway is glass.

That she blooms in the falling away.

That the pain starts on the feminine side
behind the eye.

That in sleep her body braces itself
as if high in a chimney or well.

That when in love she loses iron
and rhythm.

That the displacement of cells
is a fire in a darkened building

where against all expectation
her lover keeps looking for her
keeps taking her hand.

Familiar

There are things other than being human –
without echo.

I breathe each dark particle
and become a version of complete.

From her I learn to meet danger as water,
to stand transparent, to stand high or low,

to exempt myself from all but need.
It is she who allows me to kill, to sleep.

Actaeon

He walks his mind as a forest
and sends of himself into dark places
to which he cannot tell the way.
The hunt comes on and he in his nerves
streams ahead – hounds flung after
a scent so violent no matter the path
or what's let fall.
                     A burst of clearing.
Water beads and feathers her presence
as she thickens and curves.
He says words to himself not to look
but his eyes are of their own
and she at their centre a dark star
contracting to itself discarding
wave on wave on flare on fountain.
His skull erupting, branching . . .

And his blood is shaken down.
And he is all fours.
And his noise.
And his hounds.

Slow

Why did I choose not to understand
that what lay ahead on the darkening road
barely motorised and dripping pitch
was just a machine that would slow me down
and that the words WHITE LINE REMOVAL
were a practical warning not a sign?
And that the hundred miles to your door
were distance and not a journey towards
the unmarked freedom we hope for out of
action and pain. And that this was no
unmaking of a road but the slow motorised
drip of the dark sealing the dark.

Indigo Bunting

A bird that can sing itself to earth as sky mirror
as if to prove there is no fall that is not reflection.
I will not – three notes, ultra coloratura.

On a clear day, life streams violet from black feathers.
Ice takes softer shape, black feathers.
I mean I will not speak of this – this colour – again.

Night Material

Should they be watching or listening?
Two lovers at dusk tipping the fence
as if this house on stilts were a home
that had set them aside. They must learn
to measure themselves against the fade,
to adjust by increments
like the thousand bats under this roof:
dark corners now unfolding
into disturbance, even into noise.
A thousand rips and bounces
as if substance can only tear itself out.
The lovers are caught
with their tea-cups and champagne.
A thousand sips and bursts.
He feels as if he's swallowed the sun
and cannot turn himself down.
A thousand flits and swerves.
How can he contain, how can she hold him?

The Drip Torch

How I fetched up there we do not say.
A land far west and south of myself
so blatant in its growing and dying
clearance was undertaken by fire.
The night after a prescribed burn
you led us through your woods
to a place, strangely enough, of sleep.
The smoke low and still,
a lull of ash and the air a fleece
into which the last weak flames
knitted themselves then disappeared.
As if some great truth had occurred
and we could rest now. How glad I was
when you handed me the drip torch
and taught me how to tend fire
like a gardener with a swing of the can
across anything left untouched,
each soft splash igniting
white as a conjuror's dove
subsiding into the earth
making safe the black path.

The End of Marriage

Night was and they swayed into it:
a pair of scissors, of sails
turning only into themselves
more other than become.

It is often five o'clock.
Her husband has contracted not
to speak of her and she has forgotten
where to go. Where does everyone go?

Dreams of Separation

I keep leaving the room.

Each aspect or urgency that finds no place
in the current arrangement
takes itself outside.

They gather softly, like a wood, and wait.

Each night another room grows empty.
I find myself mostly outside.

The howling mansion.
The hyper-dimensional wood.

Lo-Fi

We have no choice.
It is in our particulars and variables
to write noise.

One among us, a knight,
drank his weaponry
and woke to speak swords.

He called for feathers.
Hurt by his cries
they choked him with feathers.

A stranger might think us blessed.

The Catch

When I left that house I took a key
to a door I never opened.
It's not the theme that interests me
but the variation.

So much is with me so soon
I lean towards the rest:
the needle's hesitation,
the song caught in the breath.

One day I'll learn to listen
to the city beneath the snow,
the agony in the irony,
the lover as I go.

English Lullaby

I have filled the day with dreams
and now must sleep.

It's hard to find the dark when darkness
has no keep.

I live the world too fast, too far,
virtual, residual.

The world is versions, fast and far,
secondary, several.

This island of sky
is filled with signs and arrows.

Each glance in the mirror
opens a window.

I take a pill to cure me
of the speed of light.

I take a drink to fix myself inside
what's left of night.

Silent Disco

She's dancing to a song you can't hear,
to inner signals rather than noise.
They give such pure direction
for once there is an only way.
She's not listening. Something's arising,
a thought that has to be kept moving,
a place in herself that was once so full.
You think you know her by that gesture,
the flick and twist of her hand as it lifts
to catch at her nape as her head tips sideways
but this is routine – a move perfected
while she was waiting, long and quietly,
for someone to let her in.
There followed the summer of dancing
out in the dark beyond the last houses
among the sneaking holly and dogwood
in a breezeblock creosote prefab temple,
by day a world of jumble and cordial,
by night a heaven of line and ring.
The look on her face is filling the room.
Someone else would describe it as *joyful*,
only to you it is space she is taking
and you will never have seen her so clearly,
so within, she forgets herself as seen.
She is pure direction, she is line and ring.

The Messenger God

How do you know?
He is ahead and to the quick.

What impression?
Grave, fissile.

Easily divided?
In that he responds.

His message?
His presence. No other message.

To what purpose?
Glass in a city of water and sky.

What need of him?
I must enter the city.

To what purpose?
Water and sky.

Hevenyssh

There is no place as airy and dilute
as level or simple.

The earth once believed
without curve or spin.

So open a view
that our presence is retraction

no more than salt
a surface concentration

or resting density – marram or pine.
I bring, I do not know, my nature:

a low pull beyond reach
a slow rush into and into.

How sun is drawn down.
How water solves each length of sand.

And the sky – so vast a gesture
lifts me from my heart

as doth an hevenyssh perfit creature
that down were sent in scornynge of nature.

Maeshowe

The year's contraction.
Sun rolls, sky rises and is long gone.

Not to see the framing steepness
you lower your head.

You are line:
a form of utterance from last to next

no more than murmur
as light pulls into the seed of itself

a held breath
your body an earthbound chamber.

Why rush past into whiteness?

This is the time of the dark half,
the serpent days of seem.

Scribbles of lust and brag
speak like needles on the skin.

Fal Estuary

The night train's chain of events.
What could be brighter?
Window by window

shocking and invisibly connected
as if we travelled on our nerves.
At the end of the line

a milky geography of salt and chalk
seaweed caught in the arms of an oak
a streaming field

where a hare starts out of the earth
wheels like a girl woken and told
to *surface*. Now? *Now*.

The hare, the girl
break up into a dance
of unready yellows and greens.

Blakeney Point

Such constancy is no celebration.
Under this careful light
it is only earth we walk on.

The long day empties.
The small things, so vital, quicken and fly.
Already no song in the garden.

The fires we build along the northern edge
are no more upsetting to the air
than breath. Is this love?

A cure for the visible.
Fern seed gathered this midsummer midnight
would render us as clear.

Severn

When the weather comes always and sideways
it's not enough, the settling.
Why is this known only and over as first
and not all over again?

Each time the tide overtakes itself
what's worked loose is moved inland
on river over-running river
carrying off the tree-chimney-telegraph
wreckage of your way home.

It starts with a lapse, a taking back
of background (breeze and creep and song)
a making room for the massive collapse
of distance, a rolling-up of the world
into a wave that comes to an end unbroken.

There's no way home. Ask the man
who turns in his sleep reaching past
his wife for his lover, his lover for his wife
and cries that the lamp must be put out
and puts it out, setting fire to his hair.

We Will Have None of Them

Come summer's end
in a land sufficiently rumoured
two daughters of the town
took on a silver atmosphere.

They lit the streets,
coat simple, eyes enamel,
hair twisted and frothed
as if sawn from tree or ice.

The people opened their doors in wonder.
Of what were these creatures?
Silk and tassel, snow and gold,
crystal and moon?

And the people were troubled
by a spell so gentle,
a deep remembering,
so dreamy, so piercing . . .

Two daughters of the town,
coat simple, eyes enamel.
They sleep now in gentleness,
in tree or ice.

Water for Tea

The question must be travelled fully
like the missing storeys of the Unfinished Palace,
a century of incompletion and its reputation made.
The air above its low roof scintillates – empty paper or glass.

How to wait with good heart?
No one can speak of it. Tonight, all talk is of the moon,
so proximate, so described, shadows foliate its surface.
It is a press of leaves, an unearthed green

to be reconstituted as light is from destination.
The question must be travelled fully. It is ten years since,
on the Tokyo metro, my train stopped for a minute
at Water for Tea Station. A warrior rested at the spring.

I remember only the bowl (geranium) and the moon,
a disc of satsuma powder-paint. As to the water,
the weather or what he said, I am certain of nothing.
To this day, I drink tea with him.

Einstein

He built a sentence as he would a house of cards.
His father's compass proposed the invisible.
The world rushed into telephones and streetlamps.
Electromagnetism was the family business.
At sixteen he finessed a paper on the state of the ether.
He admired the scientific as an insistence on standing apart
but found himself too close or too much alone.
He professed a lack of imagination
but a disposition towards abstract thought.
He conceived reality without fixture
and in contemplation, emptied himself of himself.
He put ideas into words as if addressing an envelope
and slipped past mathematics till he needed it.

Traces and External Signs

A withdrawal from form
like the lock of hair found sewn
inside your uncle's waistcoat pocket,
the inherited made strange
by its unrelatable colour.

Did you slip the suit on?
And if so did you breathe differently
as if equipped with an aqualung,
ladder or canister of oxygen?

Joy and Difficulty

To move freely, to come back early,
to pitch camp on a shingle spit,
to sleep through the coming loose
and so accumulate to one end
while unmaking ourselves at the other
as if it were possible to do this
without drawing on old for new.

A Dutch Landscape for Isla McGuire

I was telling you what Fromentin said
about walking around inside the painting
when, half-blind, you pulled out a spyglass
and settled at an irrelevant distance.

Two weeks later when we said goodbye,
your gaze sought me inside myself
like someone peering through a telescope
across dark fields.

You saw your patients through their sleep
as if the body, now unframed, were space
unfolding into space, field on field.
And somewhere in the dark, the child.

How long the sky retains its brightness
when sky is so much of it.

I Am Taken to the House of Flight

We should have travelled by air or water.
The land is nothing and the road slow.

A roof cut from the reeds by the door.
They cushion everywhere I look
and double in still water.
I would draw them as rapid noise.

Every room is lined with birds.
As my passage becomes habitual
I gather unlikeness.

Small matters of the rim of the eye,
angle or pinion, flash or crest,
a drab head.

None is as loud as its name.
Not one will call
or look any place I can follow.

Sky-faded
they are reversing out of themselves
as birds break up into reed and water.

This is the place strongest in him.
In the built night, he cries out.
Here he sleeps as on the wing.

In winter the carpets are rolled away.
Water sits by the door.

What can I tell you?
That he has brought me somewhere loosely made.
That we sail quietly across the surface.

A Theory of Infinite Proximity

Among the discussions of love
I glimpse a constant
so natural, so brightly framed
that love becomes as clear
as the first thought of an idea.

To always be about to take
a step into the other's arms,
open, hopeful, lightly framed,
a gesture made towards idea
answered in its coming clear.

As boundless in its starting point
as reflection, laughter, river,
all the world inside its frame
and visible as light defined
by more than space and time.

For one to leave and cross the world
is to move no more than past
the other, never out of frame
but here in place, now in time,
boundless, bright, defined.

Ah –

Cloud low on the low land,
such squeezed light
is more than we ask for,
no world but white.

I need the green shadows,
grey water, blue meadows.
How can I be here
when here is so bright?

Spill

Full moon. September.
Overcast. Light wind.
Five whiting, an eel.
Slight sea with a bit of colour.

No thousand boats.
No particle writhe of the shoal.
The herring is a silver purse,
no longer a purse of silver.

We breathe the fissured air
and walk where we are left to.
The empty sea agrees with the empty harbour:
a silver cloud is not a cloud of silver.

Haze

We walk the golden way, my love,
where bitter waters run.
We gaze into the overloaded view
and soften.

Like the fields, give up your shape,
become uncertain.
Be neither his nor hers, my love,
be mine, unbutton.

The yellow heat of marigold,
saxifrage and celandine
is not what burns your throat, my love,
just what fills your mind.

Blues (That's another Sunday over)

Two minutes to five, turn it up.
Fire, food and comfort? Never enough.
What little opened has long since shut.

Coal burns back down into earth
taking with it whatever worlds
might have been seen in its embers.

Scenes from a novel. Dust falls.
The page won't turn, the stranger won't call.
A town that's sinking sinks us all.

The one road out heads towards sunset.
The young drive as if overtaking death
and the old as if following the dead.

The sky bog-black by now
and my mind black by now
and the rain by now, the rain.

Otolith

A bear waking in Siberia
breathes out the last of winter
and the wind rolls west:
pine bend, reed sway,
sea plunge, sea fray,
sluice dribble, crab snap,
a merchant's Flemish beaver hat,
tooth rattle, jet boom,
curlew splash, cathedral tone,
dog confusion, jackdaw bluff,
the passing bells, the plunge and fray,
sea bend and sea sway,
the passing birds, the Flemish bluff,
a bear's loose tooth, sea breath,
corncrake, godwit, stonechat,
which of them is coming back,
the last of winter, gasp of spring,
and earth, and air, and rain.

Song

Night, and the rush through empty air.
How small each burst, how held in place,
how we wait for just such a rush of scenes,
how I try to be in more than one window
when you look up and the train goes by
too fast to read. How can you see me,
small in the rush through empty air,
so small in the stream of window light?
Look up, my love, don't read the words.
You know the words. They're not my words.

The Lost Letter

When this train
When this train gets in
When this train gets in I'll find
When this train gets in I'll find us
When this train gets in I'll find us a room

Whiskey and Scarlet Geranium

Consider this leaf. Is it not the exact suspension of whiskey and scarlet geranium we saw in the August visitation of Mars? True believers, we threw ourselves down on the sand to observe. By then our days on the island were a tide of brightness. We lived in each moment, carried nothing from one to the next. The gods issued warnings, flung stars, punctured the moon, combed lightning through my hair and on our last night staged an invasion. Their chariots flickered and loomed on the horizon. We gathered to watch, offered nothing but laughter in greeting this new delight.

On the Mountain

To travel the world explicit
in its fault and fold.

To enter the background
as each thought discards itself:

pine-needles to the tree-line,
scree beyond.

To move small, sleep low
and dream new depths

of emptiness and order.
To be troubled by neither.

The loosening air
concentrates your blood

and your heart has the simple grip
of speedwell or gentian.

You forget what it is
to elaborate or qualify.

You breathe
white against white sky.

A Circle Round Our House

Because we do not live together, we describe a circle
round our house. Like the unpaid milkman
we hurry past, walk hard to the sea wall.

No view, but a ladder. It slopes so far back
we are forced to climb over ourselves
as if growing out of some kind of shell.

Late December, the life between
one year and another. Each day,
an abandoned projection on the flattening sea.

An anchor caught in the mud keeps hold of nothing.
By what kind of arrangement?
It might as well be anchoring the earth.